THIS COLORING BOOK BELONGS TO:

KOKO heart

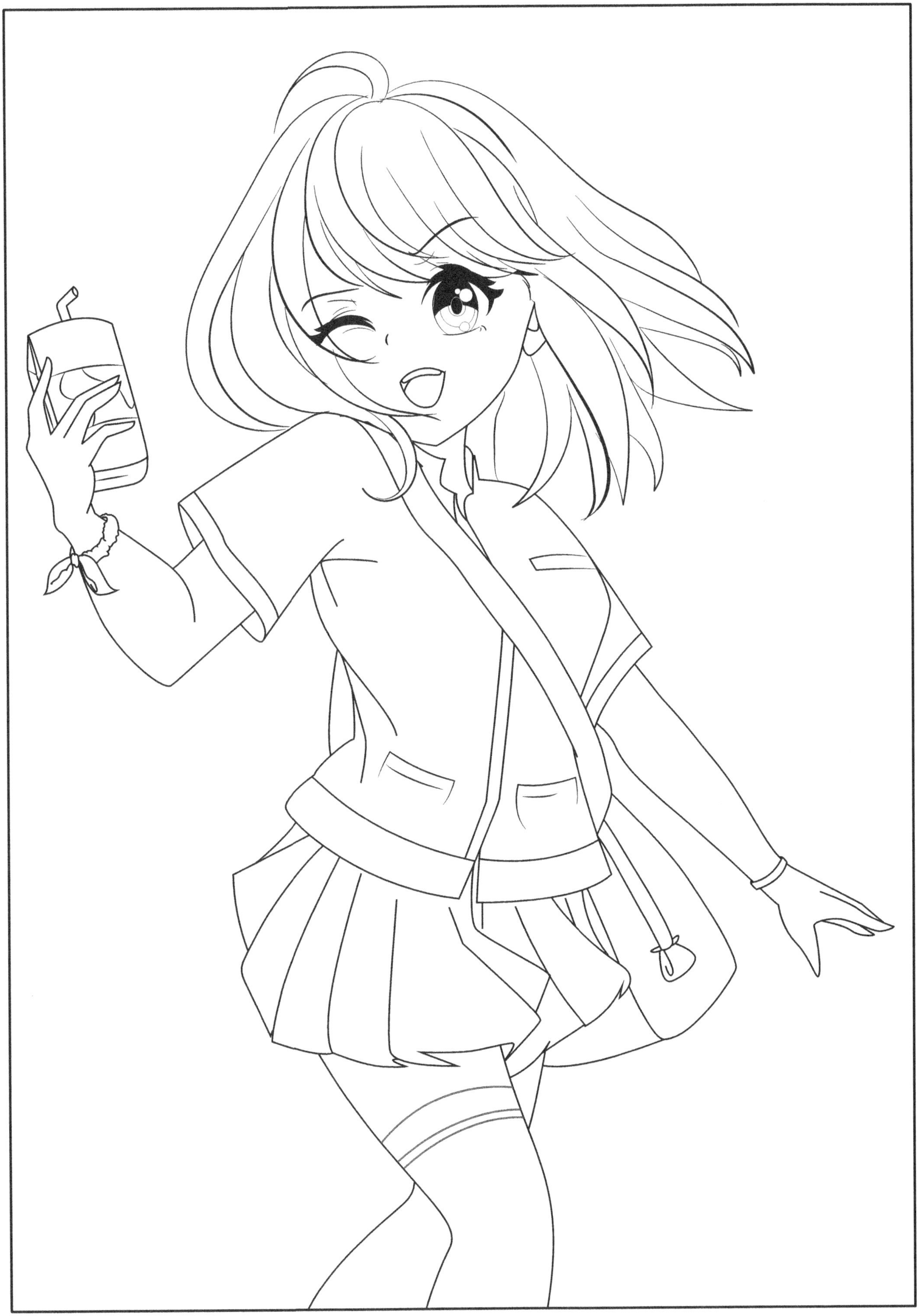

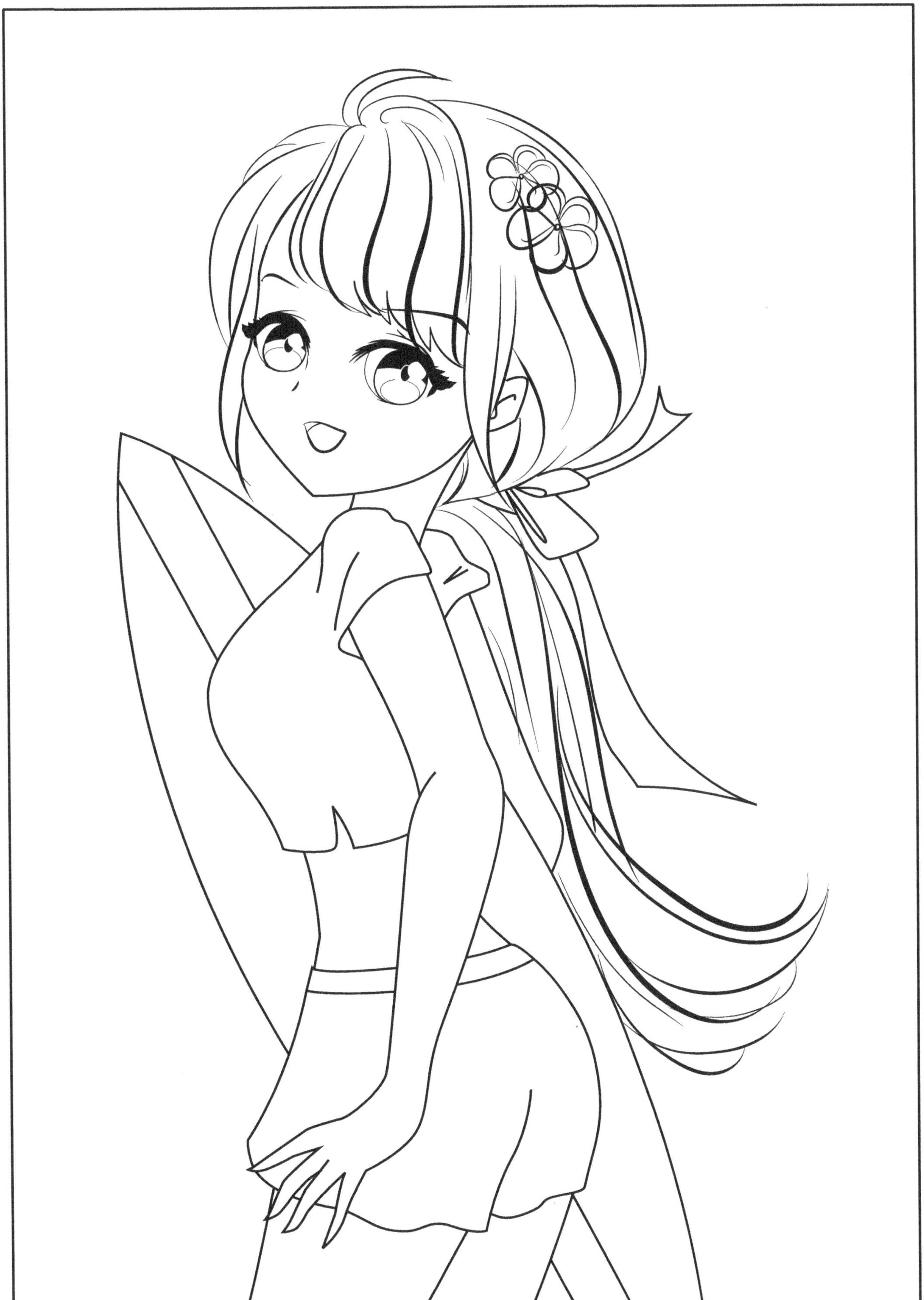

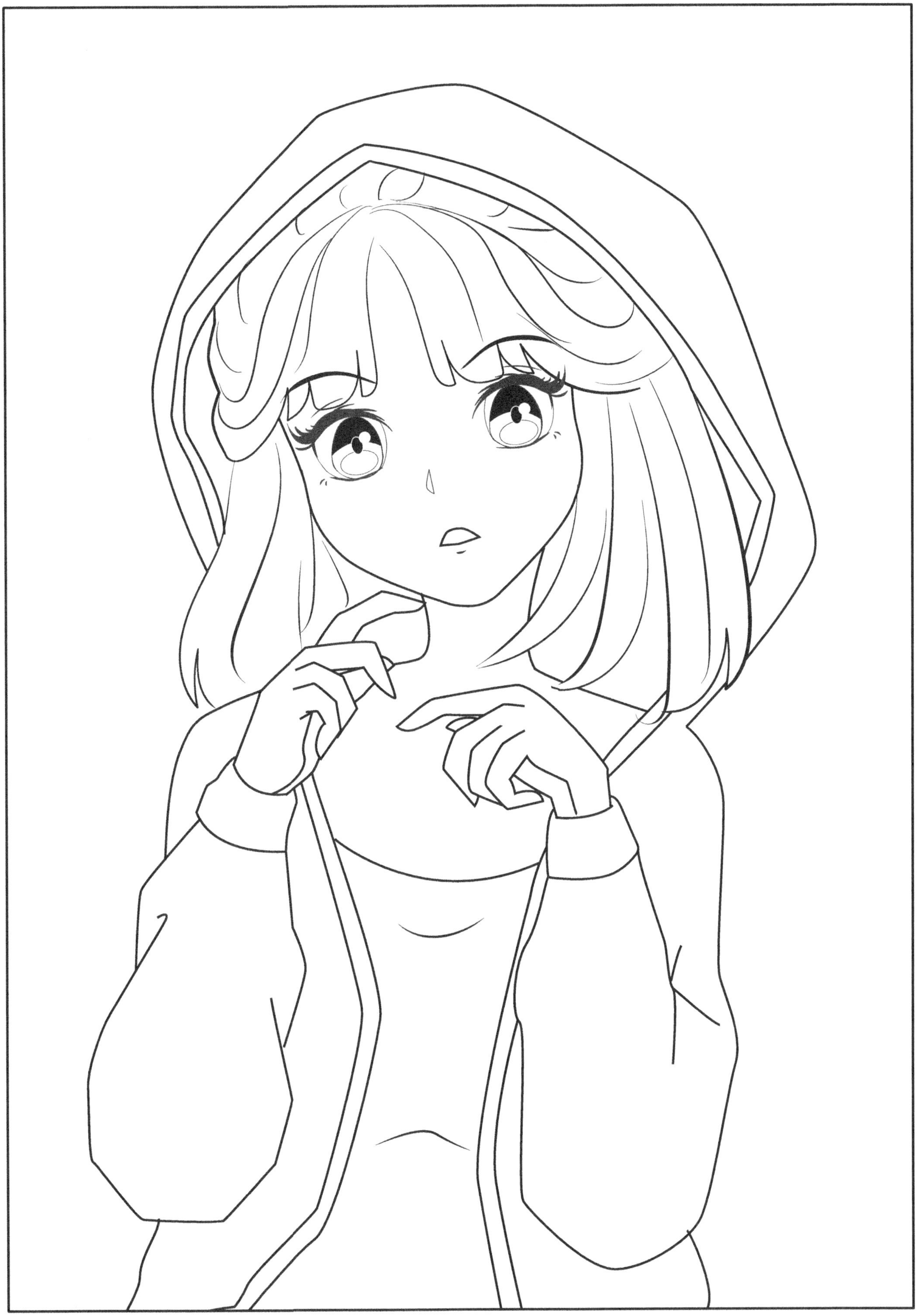

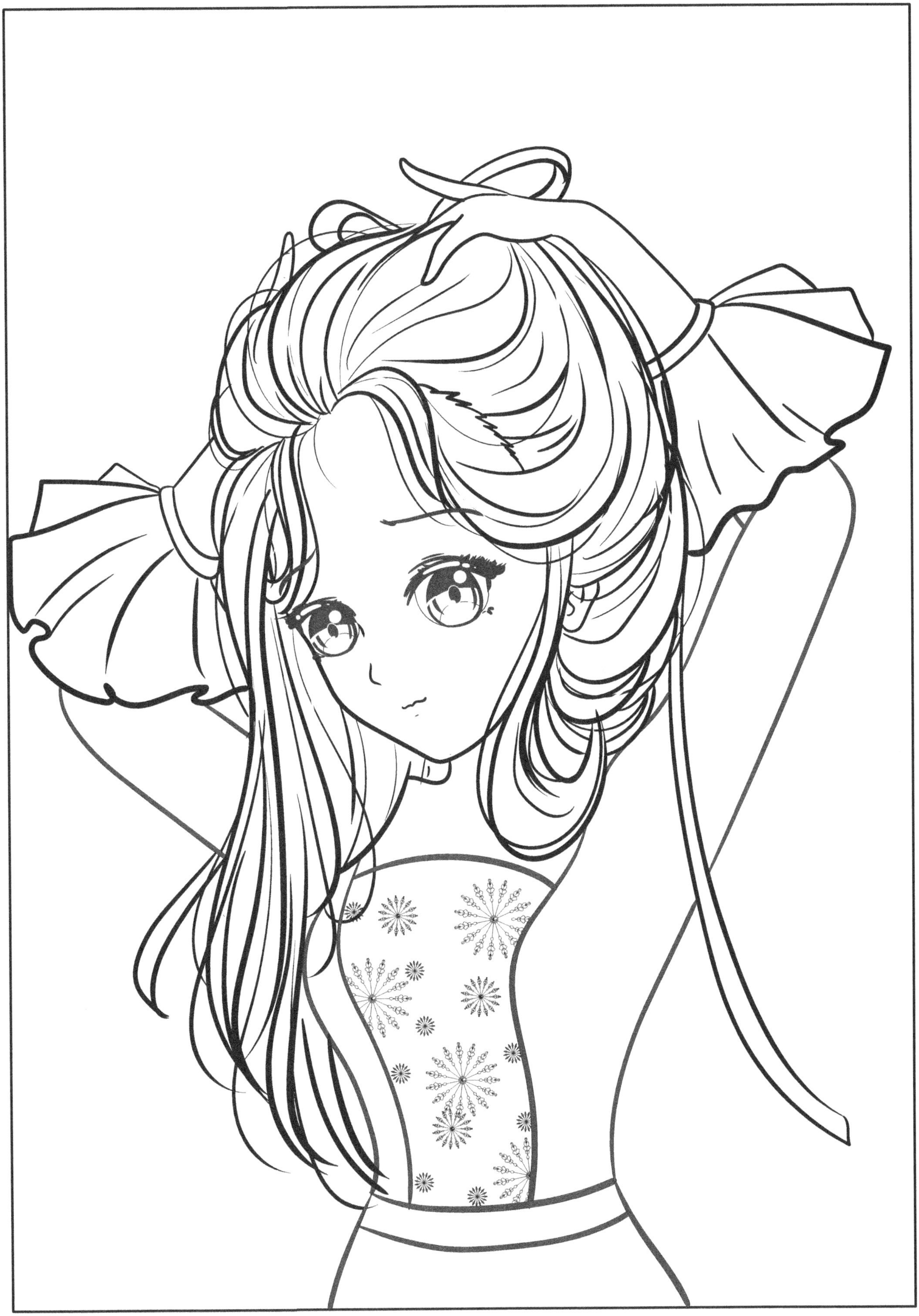

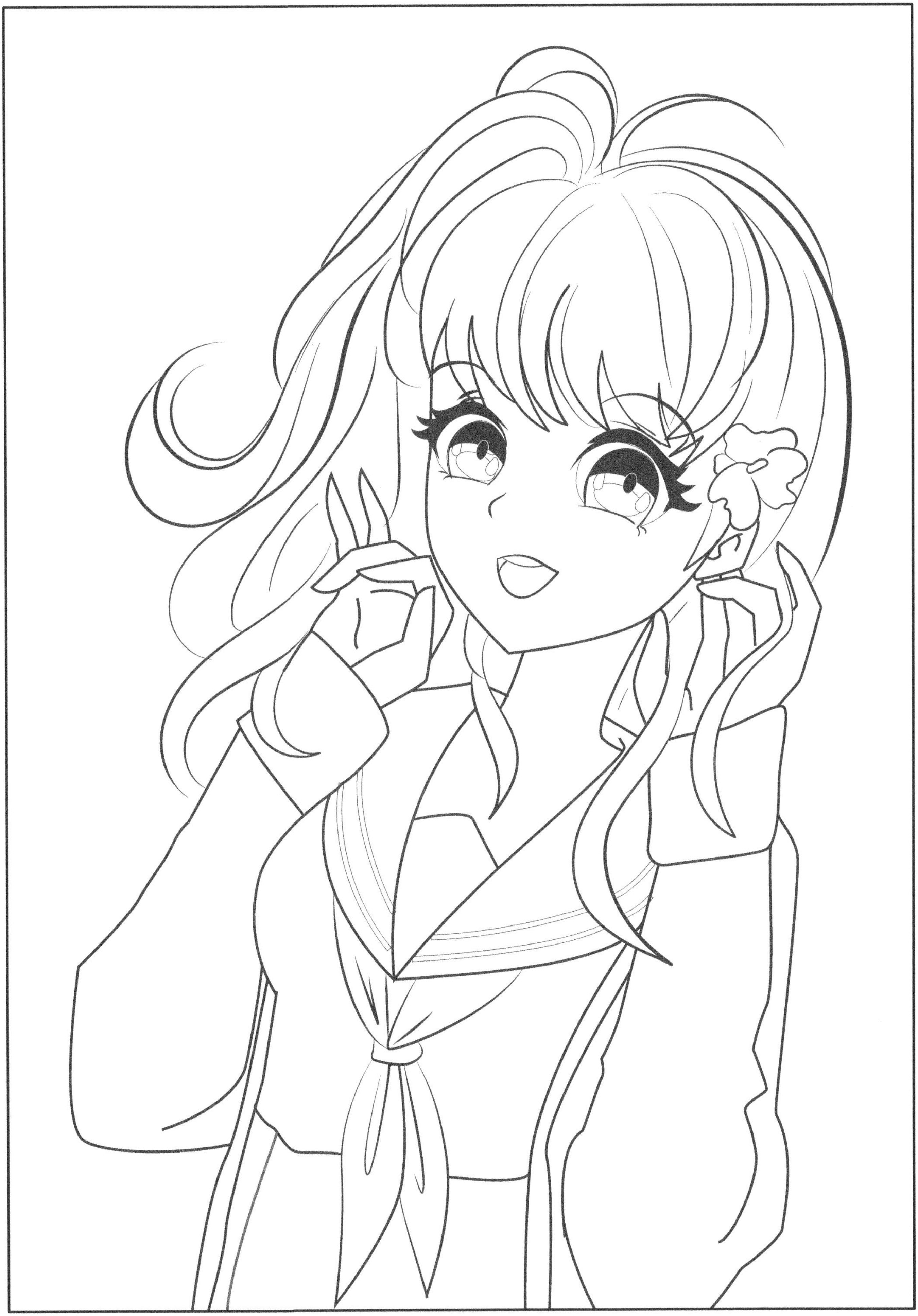

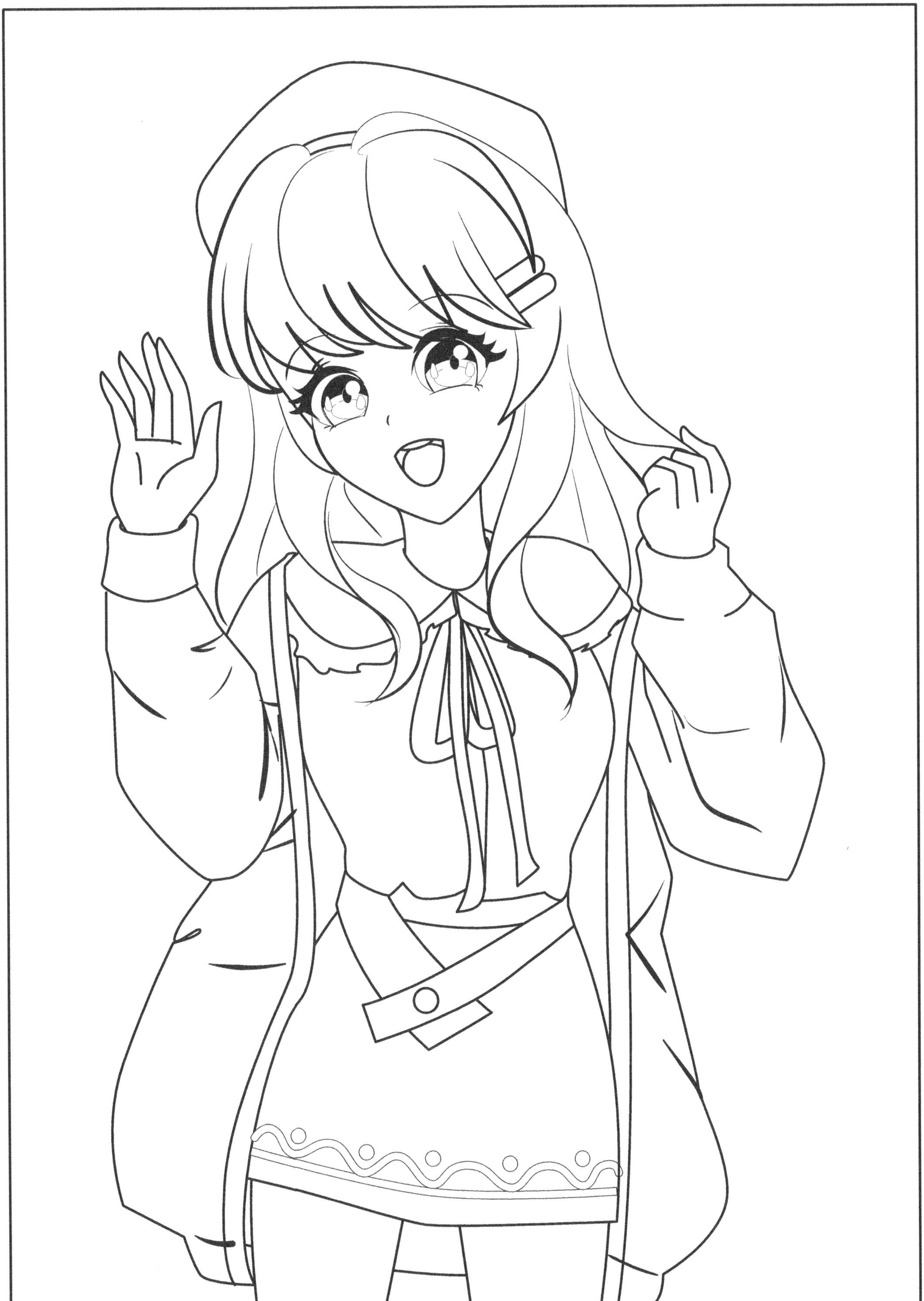

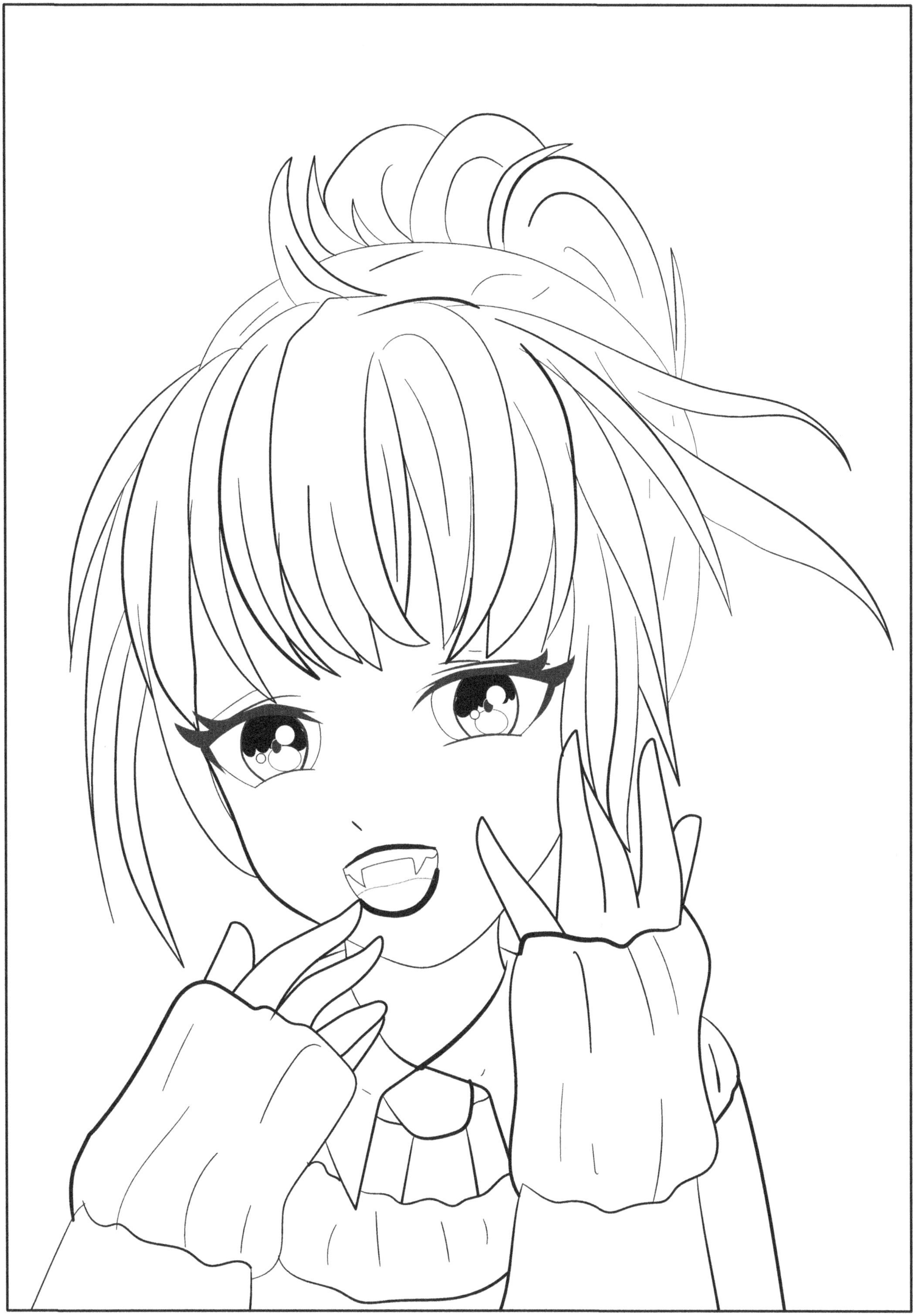

Made in the USA
Las Vegas, NV
17 January 2025

16537337R00057